Blood Memory

Blood Memory

by

Neile Graham

BuschekBooks

Canadian Cataloguing in Publication Data

Graham, Neile
    Blood Memory

Poems.
ISBN 1-894543-01-7

    I. Title.

PS8563.R323B66 2000   C811'.54   C00-900509-9
PR9199.3.G677B66 2000

Front cover image: **Anne Brigman**. *The Storm Tree*, 1912. geletin silver print. Courtesy Susan Ehrens.

The opening quotation © 1993-2000 **August Wilson**. Used by the kind permission of the author.

Quote from Robin Skelton's "Death" © 1997 **Robin Skelton**. Used by the kind permission of the Estate of Robin Skelton.

Printed in Canada by Hignell Book Printing, Winnipeg, Manitoba.

BuschekBooks
P.O. Box 74053
35 Beechwood Avenue
Ottawa, Ontario KIM 2H9
Canada

The Canada Council | Le Conseil des Arts
for the Arts | du Canada

BuschekBooks acknowledges the
support of the Canada Council for the Arts for
its publishing program.

For all of her, especially
Shelagh, Christina,
Jocelyn, Catriona, Rebecca

& for Jim

I began to see myself as a conduit of antecedents. I placed myself on the line. People say to me, "What gives you the right to write about 1936?" Nobody. I take the right. It's all part of the blood's memory. You just open yourself up to it. When your back is pressed to the wall you go to the deepest part of yourself, and there's a response—it's your great ancestors talking. It's blood's memory. In writing, I try to tap into that well, I try to tap into that part where ancestors are talking. I believe it exists.

—*August Wilson*

By the desire that loosens the limbs a woman has a gaze that is more liquefying than death.

—*Alcman*

Contents

I.   *Elemental: A Prologue*

RECONSTRUCTING A LIFE

In what way will the soul
reenter the body,
the story come alive?

First the voice naming
calling her home: child, woman, crone,
I call you back,

name you *Mairie*,
call you back to put flesh
on these bones,

to make a story
out of nothing at all.
I wish you back,

my longing a rush of wings
around your long sleep
wind through the feathers

reassembling you,
drawing the bits of you
out of the dust.

And now you're here, I say come home,
put a roof over the stones
of this tumbling cottage

carry the nettles like sheaves
away from the fireplace,
work how your body

still remembers it done.
Place your furniture
back where it stood

(your sisters, your husband,
the babies that lived)
place them

where you'll trip over them
when you should.
It's a little crowded this house,

you'll sing and I'll see it
the stones rising to the roof,
peat in the fireplace,

the kettle singing,
you happily tapping the child's hand
away from the oatcakes.

The shape of your life
in days you want to remember.
But what I've done places you empty,

a bit of wind of dust yourself
alone in this shell of a home
the cold wind rising

stirring the nettles like memories
a low moan scattering crumbling mortar,
the stones that won't stand where they should,

the history of the house fallen down,
your children fleshless themselves for years.
It is this I've called you back to.

This tale of your full life
in the emptiness now,
your human history

a ghost in the house,
fences fallen, land abandoned
all that you did here

the life that you lived
here undone
and beginning again.

ONE. *Where She Begins*

REMNANTS 1

Tomb of the Eagles, South Ronaldsay, Orkney
c. 2000 B.C.E.

item: skull, female
crown bowed by long use of a carrier strap
a string of beads broken into the tomb's fill
eagle bones
knife
sherd marked by fingernail

hers

WAYS TO TRANSCEND THE SPIRITUAL

I took the flower the child gave me,
not quite buttercup, a weed from
the lawn nodding sunlight into the grey
spring day, something I didn't know
I wanted. I took it, greedy,
because it was given with a wish
to charm, because it was a home
for my imagination: glass, a stone,
handfuls of grass, a nameless flower.

I wasn't watching, really. We were
talking. He kept bringing me more
bits of grass and then something
cold on a leaf, small and moving,
so I had to look—tiny, slow,
a slug folding away from the grasses,
drawing away from fear of the blades
touching him, not knowing what he'd
ridden into my hand. Such tiny life
moving across my palm.

I gave it back to the grasses.
The child curious I would return
a gift, let it be hidden again
in the bounties of the world,
but the flower I kept
because I could watch its beauty fade,
and the grasses I kept to guard it,
to compare. And the stone, though I have
stones in my garden already.

A child's gift, this grass, this flower,
and a live thing chilling my hand, small
as a drop of rain, a leaf of thyme.
What is small and beautiful and
therefore evil, small and beautiful
and therefore good.

MAP OF THE ANCIENT WORLD

She hesitates between
the well and the house
as she carries the bucket over
the dust-dry clearing. Beads
of water lick out from
the bucket's seams, thicken
and fall, gather the soil
into figurines.
She imagines them rising,
creatures legion and small
as scorpions.
The sun sears her bared
shoulders, raises and dries
a veil of sweat. She shrugs
and raises the bucket
slopping a new animal
brown and tiny into the world.
She is careless and tired
leaving a trail of imagination
behind her, parading
in the unmapped dirt
tygers, continents, chimeras.

PARABLE OF THE HEADWATERS

Here where wind
and sun scree
down the mountain:

the knife-cut of water scrapes
snow melt to rain,
pelts into ravine's shade.

Stones in the stream bed
play water like lute strings,
the pulse of light shaped to song.

Hunters stop on this bank to forget
their hunt, but once they have drunk
they sing down the bears to slake

their winter's thirst here, the wolves
to wash their snouts free of the blood
of deer. The water vibrates

a harp in their bones,
envoy of wind and sun
so close to the marrow.

THE MAN'S DARK VOICE

Once you dream it
something happens.
Even on the dark
face of the cliff, he
breaks from rock, tears
his bones from fissures,
ribs from stone ribs.

Open sky channels
into his mind. Striding
newly down into the valley
of night slung low
from the hills, his eyes hold
the first light he sees.
His hands crumble at your door.

Underground the world is larger:
the bones of my city
are the earth's ribs, and shake
with breath. The ceiling
is the nearest sky, stars
are touchable, sparks that slide
from my arms to my belly.
It makes light with small fire
and I hold it still.

The dark room
tightens. His voice echoes
as though shifting
through tunnels. The air
is clothed with dust
and the man's broken hands
hold flame.

Even after he has left
you don't dare say
it was a dream. A man's shape

scars the cliff's base
and his story
shapes you, keeps you tracing
the dark hills for tunnels,
while light from your window
burns toward the cliff.

ALCHEMICAL DAUGHTER

for Catriona

Changeable as the sky
behind her: this child

who leans over the cliff face;
storm and sun war above her,

wind batters clouds between
the banners of light. What storm

will break her and which
set her free? Her red hair

brightens then quiets
like the waves teasing

the rocks below. Her shape
a woman's, a child's, yields

like water as cloth and wind shape
and reshape her. She

is the cliff itself bending
to the weather, the weather wearing

the earth away. Sorting
the world, as simply

as a fistful of earth
might shape itself

into each pore of her skin,
as simply as she might sift

through a handful of beach stones
choosing beauty, choosing shape

choosing a weathered weight
that fits smoothly into her palm.

ALBAN EILIR: A CALLING-ON SONG

for Robin Skelton

Where are the spirits of the Druids
now? They enchanted each other
with rods of brass, metamorphosed
into lumps of stone and oak,
their spirits wafted through the air,
passing man and beast while
their bodies slept.
                        Where are
the bodies of the Druids now?
There was a rock that shone
and the wind tore sounds from it
like flakes of spells, when
the new priests shattered it
they found at its centre
not stone, not marble, not
flint, but a head, legs,
arms, a human shape.
                        Where
are the voices of the Druids now?
Their words spent on seasons
of corn and cattle, their tongues
like owls, their voices
sent into the world to earn
a charm, a fortune, a snare, listen.

II.   *Elemental: Earth*

Mairie Greets Morning (at 5)

Mam opens the shutters & sun swells
into the room lands on my face like a
sleepy cat the scent of oatmeal warms
the room so I tug off my nightgown
patient & good as Mam helps me into
my clothes *there* she pats my back & I
run out where the cow already milked
ambles into the field & Da behind
ready to haul the gate I stand beside
to show I know how the gate must
always be shut then climb on & it
flies me against the rest of the
fence & back to the latch I set it
then Da & I walk together into the
house the whole world & sun on it
behind us waiting for us to step back
out with stomachs round hearts open
for the whole day fat with the smells
of breakfast of Bessie of sun on the
fields the fire in the hearth Mam &
Da laugh at me sniffing it in so hard
my whole head is top-full with it

MAIRIE SLOW LONG PAST SUNUP (AT 15)

Bessie's tail flicks my cheek & I
come to with a start her warm flank
bristles my face & we fill the
echoing bucket for a wonder Bessie
doesn't fuss or mourn & *there* I've
got the pail away before she kicks it
I think she's relieved I finally
came but Mam is not she shook me out
of bed then clattered in the kitchen
then louder & shake again & muttering
looks till I scraped myself out of
the cozy sleepy aching into the barn
tripping over bits of hay gods how I
hate how the sun pierces the chaff in
the air raises such a reek from the
stalls knifing in my nostrils I hate
morning & all this everyday Bessie
snuffs as I lead her into the light &
she steams with it her whole hide
melting into the warmth just as last
night I did when Jamie kissed me
Jamie kissed me I stretched & laughed

THE WORLD OF THE DEAD

The attempt to attain knowledge of the past
is also a journey into the world of the dead.
—Carlo Ginzburg, *Ecstasies*

I Was A Pagan Baby

that's what I tell my Catholic friends
when they tell me long tales about nuns

and the high mystery of confession
when they talk about giving the Sisters

the change their parents could spare for
saving pagan babies   they laugh

over the pang of devotional guilt
the Sisters shook from their grasp

when they speak of pennies
spent on gumballs & pixie stix

that could instead be used to save
pagan souls   they confess to me

bittersweet still after all
these years   like the licorice

bite at the centre of the jawbreaker's
sweet coloured layers   I tell them

I was the pagan baby   I say that
so they will think they've saved me

or not   once in my teens a boy
baptised me in a downtown fountain

and all   but even that fell away
in a dangerous light like Satan

What We Have Lost

the men
with their tale of god's descent

and rise with sky-god
father and son

cutting their flesh
eye for eye

no word for the seasons' turn
nor rise of sun and moon but words only

for the rise of their own parts
and no other   no human thing sacred but

the spear of their flesh
to plow the earth with blood or

their chastity
freezing the land their

god made without the body's work but
only his mother's pain

your mother's sweat is nothing
nothing

all about Spirit
and nothing of spirit

nothing of dancing in the fields
nothing of the blood and

deliciously falling... but my mother   sweat on her thighs
says a pagan baby I was   nothing of the long night

not two years old I'd wander in the woods   that opens to day
with only a dog to guard me   nothing

she drew me home by calling the dog   of dirt or corn or weary sleep
I'd follow after   leaping   animal joy

FURIOUS

Wolverine's my unborn baby. He rides in me, a nightmare growling from my belly. He's fierce. He leaps out and grabs for strangers. He can snatch up worms for a snack, tear the yipping dog from a neighbor child's arms, rip a man limb from limb, blood flashing on his white white teeth. I look down and there he is. I look down and he's pretending to sleep.

Kathryn asked me at school how he got there. We were in the library looking at magazines when I spotted his portrait and pointed him out to her. All sly-voiced, she asked me how he got in my belly. I said, loud, so everyone stared, "Little girl, if you don't know I'm not telling you. Ask your mom how unborn babies get made." She blushed and slapped me then stalked away. That afternoon in Geography wolverine took scissors to the back of her red dress and cut it to flames. Her white white skin was showing and wolverine licked it. He would have bit her but she ran to tell the teacher and the teacher phoned Dad and now I'm in the basement again all night.

I hear the damp walls dripping. They swell with rain and fungus and snails and wolverine's pissy dreams, wet and rotten and glowing in the dark. When Dad leaves for work in the morning and we get out, wolverine and I will take a shower to steam the night's cold off our skin and boy then wolverine will be hot and luscious and ready for trouble.

Wolverine has been thinking about how to unlock the basement door or maybe scratch his way through. My nails bleed, but wolverine has claws. I know he does because last week when Tommy grabbed for my tits wolverine clawed his arm to the bone, and we were in trouble then. It was basement time. Basement and belt until wolverine leapt up snapping at Dad, his teeth just inches from Dad's face like scissors on a red dress, cutting the air to ribbons and fire. Right in front of Dad's face until he went upstairs for his beer and TV.

Wolverine has bright black eyes. They shine in the dark like a flash-light, but they're fleshlight. Sometimes when Dad comes down the basement stairs in the middle of the night wolverine will flash those eyes at him and Dad will go right back upstairs. But tonight when Dad comes down wolverine's asleep and his eyes are shut and there's nothing to make Dad go back upstairs until he's done and putting that ugly old blind worm away and latching his belt.

And wolverine wakes in the morning ready to tear daylight out of the world and there it is creeping in through the dirty window. We catch fire till we're black lightning, teeth and claws against the glass. And then we burst through it. Out into the white white air.

ANYTHING YOU SAY

Anything you say can and will be used
to make children uneasy, to make them
sleep. You tell tales to the children
dreaming of the dragon-keep where all
the pale maidens have clear eyes,
modest hair, and breasts uncovered
only in the struggle deep in the heart
of the hero (you) who takes her
from her scaly, lascivious lover. O the look
in their eyes when they wake to your
weeping, keeping sleep away—first
by the magic of your voice
and then by what you say.

TWO.   *Where She Wanders*

R EMNANTS 2

Burial mounds, Near Polrovka, Russia,
c. 5th Century B.C.E.

bent arrowhead lodged in body cavity
bronze daggers
arrowheads
swords
whetstones
legs, like the men's, angled into bowlegs
   as if astride a horse
clay and stone altars
bone spoons
seashells

a "remarkable flute carved from an animal bone"

hers

THE PROPHET AS TRAVELLER

The man who reads portents
knows everyone's name.

He knows direction: the angle
branches point in heavy wind.

When he comes to your door
offer food and a bed,

even if your daughter
goes hungry and sleepless.

If he dreams red dogs
under your roof, he warns

of fire. If he dreams long-legged
cranes stalking high grass, flood.

If he dreams your sheep
raining down from the hills, famine.

If he has dreamt nothing at all
he will read tracks a bird,

broken-winged, left below your window.
Miles down the road he'll call

your daughter's name
you'll find her bed empty.

When she returns she will not speak,
but the child in her arms will sing.

SOOKE RIVER STORY

Just past this river's yearly tide,
somewhere in June, we rest on basalt
smoothed by the river's age. Sleep

beads your skin like sweat
and when I dive into the river your hand
waves off the water spray.

Current tosses me downstream while you lie
upriver sleeping, years of leaves rotting
around you, your body abandoned,

never moving. This snow-fed river
is a different world, clear as ice,
deep in the changing light.

Trout dart in and out of hollows. From
the shadow of the bank I steal a panful
of gravel and gold. Then rising from the river,

I cut through salal along the river's bank.
The water on my arms and thighs dries into my skin.
When I find you a dream still buzzes

around your head. You taste like salt and sun
brewed over hours of light, which doesn't explain
why at first I can't wake you. This

is the kind of legend that surfaces
in your dream while the river
rustles beside you in its own hollow bed.

STORY 1

I walk home alone
at 3:00 am, night
chill, I laugh at what
the accidental
silence says to me.

How dark and sullen
the night is. Like me:
female and bleeding
like prey/a promise/
blessing/death/rain. No

child shudders from me
like a sweater down
my shoulders, pours but
reluctantly. That's
all. And what that means.

THE NAME OF THE HUNT

Fire is the name I'd have taken
to carry with me, but I stole
what I could: your bed,
warm sleep, all the easy dreams.

They've done me no good, left
nothing but hunger and I hunger
through this long winter bare
even of snow. When the wind covers

me these nights, it tells me
you've hidden in a cave to wait
for spring. I warn you
it was there wolves

found me with no fire to keep
them away; I lay with them
three nights, and now we hunt
to kill our hunger. Hunt

for the first break of spring.
You must keep moving, keep
night from your bones: when
we pause on the face of the hill,

testing the wind, it's your voice
I listen for, you and what
I couldn't carry.

S TORY 2

Summer sun malts on
skin, a flow dappled
by leaf and light till
my body is a
stream—a flow of bone

and shadow in a
bed of long grass and
weeds, the current a
pulse and stutter of
blood, slow renewal.

The breeze of your hand's
warmth slowly wakes me—
I surface to the
mixed breath of the sun,
the earth, the wind, you.

LOVING THE GREEN MAN

for Bette Tomlinson

Vines smile from the corners of his grim mouth
their fluid beauty a story   A trail

of leaves like breadcrumbs eyed by birds
but for this moment perfect   Still   Smooth face

cheeks round as the haunch of a deer   His eyes
point blankly out through the tangle around

us   The vines speak for him   An agony
of symmetrical voices tamed on his

either side   A twist of waves and spreading
branches and his face the center   What he

dreams he sees   Carved in wood   In stone   His face

changes from one church to the next   To the
fireplace in Littledean Hall   And it's the

forest that was   The man in branches   Green
and beating all over these hills   He sees

what he once was   Through us   The wild taste in
our mouths that we must speak   His clear and bitter

voice on our tongues   We're off listening
to the wind of what he needed to say

MY LOVE OUT RIDING

Sister, I met my love out riding
as he brought his bay mare to drink
from the stream. He said I froze
like a deer there crossing the water
when he stretched a hand
to lift me to the bank beside him.
The warmth of his lips
on the rough chill of my palm still
moves in my veins.

Sister, today I showed him a robin's
nest in the hedge: four blue eggs
the colour of magic, of sky, his blue
blue eyes. We walked through the woods
for no one to see. He says my black hair
is the same silk as his waistcoat, my
eyes a colour rich as earth, my
homespun pretty enough to lace
flowers through.

Sister, I met my love out riding.
He lifted me onto his bay mare
and we rode together, under the old oaks.
I showed him the foxes' lair,
the watercress by the hidden spring,
and where the raven keeps his horde.
There's a place now where the earth
and bent bracken hold the spell
of our bodies' warmth.

Sister, today we watched robins
testing their wings, learning
to fly south from the storms.
He kissed our father's stripes
on my back, my thighs, kissed
my rounding belly and pledged
his shelter, his home, a gold ring—
promises like roses I hold
whose petals I count as I
count each day.

Sister I looked for my love out riding
I found only storm, wind, rain.
Cold rain. His promises dull as torn petals
useless as thorns. But now I gather
fox paws and ravens' wings to warm
my child, I'm learning new words
the storm's fury tells me.
A new language that builds a pyre now
twig by twig.

Sister the child in my belly rages
and my heart is stone.
I am still, quiet
as the storm's heart, the heart's storm
over. My body is languid with
this child, but the fire's bitter heat
will catch, the spider will dance
in her web, my hands itch
with lightning.

Sister, I met my love out riding. His
golden wife from the city rode behind
on a dappled mare, but a black wing
sent it thundering for home and a red paw
led the bay to a spider guarding
the door where I left our son sleeping.
Now my love is stag-footed, his proud head
crowned with branches and his limbs at last
fleet in the woods.

Sister, I meet my love out riding
as I bring his bay mare to drink
from the stream. He freezes
there, wary. And when I stretch a hand
to lift our son to the bank beside me,
and my love flees beyond the thicket,
but the chill of my lips on the rough warmth
of his neck still moves in his veins.
It moves.

THE LOVERS IN GREY

i Aubade

Light splays across the room: inside it two figures move
stiffly like paper silhouettes behind the screen of light, never
touching. You can't make out what it is they're doing,
as they pass each other, pass and speak, back and forth across
the stage of the room. You think perhaps they argue, wonder
if she's packing, and it burns that you can't know.
The border between their lives and yours
is a gaping street wide. What is their story?
Has the man ever held the woman's head in his hands, stroked
her hair? Has the woman ever turned to him from the window,
winter light and trees caught in her face? The room is bare,
the one lamp open as confession, the man and woman both closed
as walls. What do they say? Could she lean forward, shut off
the lamp, let daylight enter March-grey, her eyes opening like clouds?
What then over this distance would this say?

ii Evening Wind

First the woman, her skin tightening, her hands and leg
on the bed she's about to enter, but she's turned, her hair barely
stirs in wind that knocks the curtain into the room. She's turned
to look past the bricks that frame the window,
into the blank light there, wind that breaks
over her skin. Cold air pushes in from thousands of rooms
in the city around her, from the sea beyond. Across the sea
there's a shore and a city, and by a window is a man naked
where air moves outward from his skin, back to where the woman
still has not moved into bed: the wind on her face chills her.

iii Madrigal

She loves small and wild. Her face pressing
into his turning away. Her flesh damp with fear and love
and body's warmth in the night. She nuzzles into him,
warm animal waking him. She won't rest. Moves over him
approaches his other side, her hair tickles his face. Her breath
is warm on his cheek restless and light. It is love,
her anxious hands on his shoulder
nervous lips on his brow. It is love here
running swiftly away.

iv Winter or Goodbye

Here, tonight, well near sleep she stumbles
to his house, knocks and the door wanes
to a face he wears that is not quite his own.
She is on the outside of this demanding door.
But she asks only that he walk with her once
out into the dust falling snow.
He dons boots and scarf and his own face
and they walk out into the sky, solid with snow
and the held city light. Each streetlight a world
and the snow grinds at their steps announcing them hushed
to the next angel of light sharpened
by the maple's bare branches, but thickening, dull
with snow. It falls on them, melts into them
through their cold-thinned skins, freeing them
from the weight of their wet clothes. Her hand
when it finds his is warmer than fire, leaves him
at his door, and she's drunk with ice
with this white-bound world with the turn
of her tracks in the snow.

III.   *Elemental: Air*

M AIRIE IN THE CITY MORNING (AT 25)

Gods the clank of traffic outside &
men shouting merchandise into the
storerooms & I queenly at my
typewriter lining up words & with
them I scatter men & boxes into
trucks all over town the scent of
exhaust & bitter coffee scatters me
around the late morning room till the
sound of doors & voices raised
punctuates my keys' clatter & here's
the boss in a mood handing me a sheaf
of papers *there* he says *what's that* &
all I can do is laugh at the note
slipped in there amongst the daily
letters & Jamie's cologne bites up
from the page & the scratch of his
words I shake my head then the boss
shakes his finger but he smiles & I'm
back to my desk flushed with the
remembered rasp of Jamie's cheek my
lips still swollen from his mouth's
work my fingers typing his face

MAIRIE AT THE NOON HOUR (AT 35)

Jamie bursts in rings his keys on the
tin tray on the sidetable & the kids
chortle around him like birds lunch
is late as the morning skipped by me
like daughter Ellen's feet scuffing
the chalk-lined hopscotch by the
garden gate I unearth tins of soup
buried against just such a day &
rescued thereby I heat crackers to
take the staleness out & Jamie
nuzzles my neck as Ben drags from his
arm like a fishing weight *there* I
ladle the soup into bowls on the
table tear garden basil to wake it up
& its scent prickles me aware here's
Jamie Ellen Ben for this moment here
& bright all circled smiling in the
window's lemon light in the soup's
steam in the kitchen's warm bonds I
can *see* them remember each murmuring
in their sleep I know them how the
herb's green life stains my fingers

AND SEA AND THE WILD WOOD

after Kathleen Yearwood

the spiral's song

I wake caught in falling tangles
gulls scream   wheeling
as though they know me
my head crowded with birdlight
I turn to hear a song but it's
thrown in a spiral of spray—
light   wind unravels
to the lonely cadence of
an incantation from the throat
with a lullaby of feet
knotted night undergrowth
a rhythm the marrow stirs with
my tongue cannot learn to listen
against my palate   the slap
simply breath

speaking to the wind

huts of twigs and rain spin
through the dawn's light
shoes full of weeds and thorns
hands full of fallen leaves
only pebbles the waves have
I could explode with
whole cathedrals of sound
my shoes on sliding stones
of the path   open and beating
the trail open-handed   but its edge
beauty deeper than the bone
I've had enough of talking
to the wind in my mouth
of sound   and in my throat
simply breathing

THE BASEMENT EXIT

skylight   *fever*

Down here even sunlight   scuts into the corner
with tassels of dirt   and paper shreds
a torn shoe   useless   even to we drifters
who pile rage after rag   on dry bones
while clouds of waste pile   over us   covered by
weather and sheets of   rain   on one side
the walls missing   bricks garnished with
scraps of signs   and   paint   on the other
rows of doors   handleless   splinters   spiking from
the locks say   Exit Only
and otherwise the street   and   strangers with houses
lit by bulbs   and glass   and jobs
with hours and bosses   while here
the deadline is food and   numbness and where
to find it   how to pay   with flesh or spirit
and then sometimes   the dream of the headless
the usually kindly rats   and the sun   the sun
no longer filtered   through the dirt and waste
but shards of glass   passing through me
sharp as the words in   my fever
like knives   like cigarette   ends against me

THE GAME OF CARDS

The words you won't say shuffle in my head,
offer me the joker, a jack of spurns. Shuffle again,
turn up the eight of clods, thump in my head,
the trump a trumpet if ever I heard one. So now
I lay out a game of solitudes, the two of diatribes,
covered quick with the three of shames, the four
of chimes to silence it.
                    Your deal.
Cut the cards. You ask me to pick one
for the past, one for love and one for keepers.
Your hands move faster than a riverboat gambler's,
an ace slides up your sleeve and dangles there,
it's the ace the act of harm.
                         I pick the cards—
the queen of diagrams to describe my past,
then four of change for love, and last, I choose
a king, the ruler of dialogues. But you pass me
the king of shades.
                    The solitaire double now,
the game spite and malice, hearts and crazy fates.

THREE. *Where She Lands*

R EMNANTS 3

Gravestone, Elgin Cathedral ruins,
northeast Scotland

Elisabeth Paterson
Decessit 12 Aug 1698 Aetatis 36

Elisabeth here lyes who led her life
Unstained while virgin and twice married wife
She was her parents image her [days?] grace
All the illustrious honours of the face
With eminent piety and complaisance
All the decovements of exalted sense
Davids swan song much in her mouth she had
More in her of it established
Departed hence it beeing her desire
All and delight just when she did expire
By all bewailed she in the flower of age
As Jacobs Rachel was turned of the stage
Ane only child beside death by his sting
Unto this urn within three day did bring

this stone hers

REMNANTS 4

Stone in a graveyard
outside Stromness, Orkney

Sacred
to the memory of
ELLEN DUNN
who departed this life
August 3rd 1858
aged 17 years

Stop for a moment youthful passers by
on the momento cast a serious eye
Though now the rose of health may flush your cheek
and youthful vigour, health and strength bespeak
yet think how soon like me you may become
in youth's fair prime the tenants of the tomb

this stone hers

GRAVESTONES AT ELGIN CATHEDRAL

The words sing in the brain.
  Words did I say? No, worms,
    twisting, mumbling *memento*
mori, the hourglass run out
  on weathered stone, grasses
    humming beloved spouse, dead
23, 39. Women known best
  for piety, that's what counted
    when you were buried beside
your infant daughters and sons.
  So what's a life, a story,
    a memory, the tale we can
never know even if she could
  tell it. The skull and bone,
    wyf of, daughter of, the box
and the spade, who remembers
  these voices, knows the songs
    that filled their mouths,
knows how little this piety
  holds, the truth
    of the skull's arc
the lies written on stone.
  What is mourning 300 years on,
    when the rain has obscured
her name, her youth, the words
  her family sought comfort by.
    Cut grass pools in the hollows
of the stone, moss gathers
  in the etched lines. Love
    is perfect now.

THE SKIN OF OUR TEETH

i *from the northern mainland*

The sky spits down rain
     into the mud of the fields,
even the goats huddle together
     for warmth. My daughter's
dirty fingers slip from my hand

and she jumps in a puddle splashing
     her skirts, thinks I don't see her
behind me. The babe in my arms
     stirs and settles as the rain
hits his cheeks and I smooth

the blankets to shelter his face.
     The drops shaken from my sleeve
disturb him again. We're climbing
     down from the headland
where we watched the ships

sail out and away, watched
     their father set out west
the high proud serpent on their prows
     singing rough warnings to the wind
in their teeth. My husband sings.

Wisps of his husky voice blew over
     the jagged rocks of the headlands
proud—though he never looked our way
     before the other men—
of the man-child in my arms

and the one that will soon
     stir in my womb. The one who died
from the flux while he last sailed
     now forgotten, like our first,
the daughter, who coughed blood

in the middle of winter, whose body
       we had to wait until thaw
to bury. Their father.
      I try not to think of him
now that he's gone, though my thighs

still sting with his farewell.
      I would jump in the sea
to wash this blood clean. Maybe
      I'm losing this child.... I grab
my daughter's hand, pull her

alongside me from her dawdling
      play. Try not to think
of the pain that makes walking
      uneasy. Try not to think
of the other women my husband

has chafed against; those
      on the raids I try to think of
least of all, whether he cuts
      their throats before or after—
before or after he's killed her man,

before or after he takes
      the girl-child too, before or
after he's thrown the babe
      from her arms. If it's true
that nothing will grow

where anyone has suffered, that
      nothing will grow where anyone
has died, that western land
      would already be a barren place,
with no riches to draw my husband.

But blood makes for fertile
      soil. Look, the ravens already gather
along the trees by the shore,
      one follows me home.
My babe opens eyes wide with hunger,

mouth searching for my breast.
     I give him my braid to suck,
for with the new child coming
     my milk has gone dry. He mouths
my hair in disbelief,

his sky-blue eyes so wide
     his mouth open and crying, squalling
his pink mouth open wide enough
     to swallow all the riches of the world.
I give him my empty breast,

nothing else to offer.
     He gums it till it bleeds,
like the woman on the western isle
     I have nothing to offer
but a breastful of blood. My daughter

slips from my hand. The raven
     cawing, the rain and cold wind
from the sea on my skin.

ii *from the western isle*

News of the northern raiders
flies up the coast.
The skittish priests
have already gathered
their skirts and crosses,

buried what they could not
carry and fled inland.
We stay with the fields
as they ripen toward harvest,
my father and brothers

work to keep the crows
off the corn and share
lookout on the point.
I've had my turn there.
Always fearing each speck

against the sky will be
their serpent-headed prow.
There's not much here
—the empty church
the beasts in their pens

the immature corn, the crows.
They'll take it all, take
or ruin. But when they
come, I'll not hide.
They can take all our treasure,

ransack my home.
I'll hide the baby
then come to fight,
cleave a skull
or two with the best

of the men if I can—
and if it comes to the worst
and one throws me to the ground
I've made a vow
to the old gods of blood

and power. I'll offer
one last prize
for the raiders—a
quick thrust of the knife
I keep warm against

the flesh of my breasts
like a child. He won't
feel it, the gentle slide
of a tongue of fire
beneath his skin.

THERE AS HERE THERE ARE NO DOORS

My daughter is only four
and I cannot find her.
There was a pile of crumbling
concrete from the wall
where we had hidden and
everything under it
broken—I cannot think of it,
I would like a little water. Please
don't ask me to lie still.

—

Tell my neighbour
if her house is still there
to tell my husband where
I am. Tell her not to look
for my daughter. She was hiding
from the noise against the wall
nearest the river.
Water, please.

—

It tastes like water should,
not like the river
we boil when we have fuel to burn.
They wanted my oldest son for a soldier.
He looks older
than his years, nearly the age
of the ones they take.
He and his brother
are never parted.
They bring me treasures
from the rubble, metal
from fallen planes.
They would like to fight
—who would not like to shoot
these carrion birds from the sky,
bury them under the fallen
stones of our city. Let their
mothers dig them out.

STORY 3

she said she didn't
know why said no she
hated him even
when he tore his clothes
in his hurry to

touch her said it was
hate still the moment
his tongue said even
then she said even
hate as he whispered

beggings in her ear
yes she said still but
sometimes said sometimes
his touch said sometimes
lust softens our bones

NETTLE WIFE

I'm tired of being silent
for you in the other room, tired
of watching the night
settle closer. The cat chases
white petals
          blown against the windows
from the cherry tree outside,
just as months ago in the storm
he chased snow.
          He chirps,
his paw slips on the glass
and down. The tree outside
shines,
      white clouds
in the evening's black branches.
The tree glows dark
          against
darker skies. I want to tell you
about what the spring wind
might bring,
         fires lit
against midnight sky—
sparks
      and stars in the darkness.

IV.   *Elemental: Fire*

MAIRIE IN THE AFTERNOON (AT 45)

quiet now but the house still throbs
with remembered furor Ellen & Ben
wrangling about the car their stereos
dueling across the hallway while her
probationary perfume battled his
abandoned socks these days Ellen
dreams of dark men Shakespeare Van
Leeuwenhoek Descartes while Ben toys
with soccer balls oil paints the
long-haired girl next door all of
their noisy growing suddenly paused &
they are their own solitudes now
still our blood & making but they're
building bonds that aren't to us damn
these days I think too much quiet now
quiet there's Jamie & Ben in the
garden tucking the plum tree just
there as Ellen buries the roots & I
with mint tea & an ink-dusty book
settle by the old dog & the basking
cat sit in the window legs up looking
out mistress for now of all I survey

MAIRIE SERVES DINNER (AT 55)

a thrust of wind & old friends Kate &
Mark arrive with woodsmoke to incense
their coats moth balls echoing rasp
from their scarves newly unstored   I
cook & we eat then Jamie pours musty
fruity wine & I fetch crackers &
veiny cheese & old friends we've told
our stories so often but we describe
the turbid rain in some far travelled
place the dusty sun in another & how
lost we were there & how found & how
new & possible the world can seem
then Mark & I alone in the kitchen he
reaches across to pick up the tray
his arm electrically *there* brushes my
breast & with one long look of wide
frightened eyes white faces I think
of Jamie's love 30 years long & Kate
mothering Ellen when I had Ben & we
know us too well we smile & duck out
his arm slides home along Kate's
shoulder my hand warms Jamie's thigh

DELICATE AS THE SHAPES OF SPIRITS

bullets in the field   *the river believes*

in a field of gray grass   I walk the river's edge
the clouded sky fierce white   rocky with your memory
as though bled of colour   and below   furious   water roars hidden
beyond my sight   it is dusk   though I can't see the sun
anywhere setting   just it seems   the light is darkening
I walk farther in   the grass   thicker and higher   but
still not lush   each blade   offers nothing   ahead of me
the far bank of cloud gathers   coalesces into a shape   a form
something nearly alive   nearly   once alive   if I knew no better
I would say it was someone they   brought to the riverbank once and
shot neatly through   the heart, who otherwise might
have fought forever   I might   wonder how they made you
stand so still that bullets   could find your moving form
with such precision   the gray of the grass beads
with rain   I am wet through   and dissolving   my mouth tastes of
ashes   of what I imagine   is the flavour of despair   but
then I stop imagining   I work so hard against belief
I am wet through and dissolving   my mouth against the wound
and ashes   but this is not despair   not something you would
let yourself say   ever fighting   for this more than anything
I hate you   for this   and that river below

ALONE AFTER MIDNIGHT

Why We No Longer Weep   *The Silence of the House*

oh but we still cry and rage   my back in the corner   furnishings
tear against pain against doubt   surround me and tick in the sun
   hating our history   a zodiac clock measures out something
the tale it tells   less than seconds   its own bars of time
of our every kind of weakness   I'm a traveller inhabiting my life
but we can't weep   we're too   like a hotel room   its fine quirkiness
      alive   the gentle consideration of the management
for that   alive and bitter   anticipating my needs and desires
      despite   shelves of books I have read and
   our sweetness—   will read the music   I'm fondest of
any man who has bitten into us   two cats with their long historic presence
will attest to that   in my days   what is it that they know me so well
it's not that we won't love   that what clamours for attention here is
the man who wants to win us   the ticking of my body
   we'll love him   in summer
till his marrow aches with it   my heart's rhythm   the hum of possession
but we won't weep for him   buzzing through the rooms
it's not because death is   constructed by strangers but
something we can't stop   inhabited with the discarded
   or that love is   cells of my flesh and ideas about
something we can let be over   but   how I want to live and
because we can't ever let it be   what the desire constructs   its
so easy let   tangible notions of
it simply end   the duties I owe to the world

THE TREE IN THE WORLD

Here it is, the easy metaphor.
The sharp, simple, (twisted) equivalency,
the words meaning death. Let me explain:
outside my window is a tree,
yes, leaves that catch and bend light,
their shadowed, secret unders, the mystery
of their autumnal transformations.
Last November after it turned,
before the brunt of winter hit it,
the landlord came with a saw and
lopped it, hacking unevenly,
not pruning but attack. Barely
more now than unsymmetrical branches
eccentrically offering their leaves
to the light, but the following spring
it sacrificed blossoms to the season.
This tree is a part of my human family.
Think of it as the poor,
attacked by the landlords, who say
I only rented to her because she
was from a rich family, they can't pay
the new rent, let them find another place,
that man. The misshapen branches,
the blossoms, the new leaves,
its awkward inelegance, its lumpish dance
in the wind. But this morning a cherry,
just in my reach. I picked it, dear listener,
and my lord it was sweet. It tasted alive.

CONSIDER TEIRESIAS

Teiresias, dull and blind as prophecy
having spied on Athena's bath or else said

for spite what Hera didn't want spoken,
is sightless. Teiresias like an old shoe,

empty and flapping his sullen tongue,
speaks the words Zeus wants to hear.

What Zeus, waxing bovine, showering gold,
shuddering his huge white wings, wishes

to believe. The empty-eyed grey old man
once proud and young, was once transformed

into a woman then a man again.
If his shape was altered by slighted Aphrodite

Teiresias was a crone, beautiful-haired.
If by the coupling snakes

he was a famed harlot seven years.
And thus Teiresias knows more

than the beefy men: what Hera knows,
what Athena does—perhaps.

Old Teiresias delights in signs,
telling the people what to sacrifice and when,

but he knows less than Actaeon
and his hounds, less than Zeus

in his animal ways. Teiresias either
knows nothing of singular passion

or else for seven years closed his eyes
or for the rest of his life his blindness

was willful, or else his prophecies
would take longer years to reach

true listeners than Cassandra's,
travel more intricate ways

than foolish Odysseus. Consider Teiresias,
once glad and big, braver than me,

bigger breasted than you,
tonguing his dead language, foul-mouthed,

flaunting his blindness,
fallen vision, his hollow chest.

FOUR. *Where She Starts Again*

REMNANTS 5

artifact-filled privy
327 Aliso Street, Los Angeles
a "parlor house"

Gouraud's Oriental Cream
Prof. Huberts' Malvina Cream
S&K Italian Cream
Dr. Funk's Cream of Roses
French perfumes,
    domestic colognes, Florida water

Calder's Saponaceous Dentine
Van Buskirk's Fragrant Sozodont
        for the Teeth & Breath

crystal liqueur tumbler
French porcelain
beer bottles & whiskey flasks

6 rubber syringes & injector bulbs
9 quart-sized bottles Darby's Prophylactic fluid
12 jars vaseline (to mix with mercury)
Ayres sarsaparilla (against syphilis)

Shiloh's Consumption Cure
    (morphine, alcohol, muriatic acids,
     extract of henbane, wild cherry and ginger,
     essence of peppermint, syrup of tar, water,
     chloroform, prussic acid, hydrocyanic acid)
California Fig Syrup
Brown's Essence of Jamaica Ginger
    (90% alcohol)

2 glass syringes
breast pump

TAM LIN

Janet green and wild
her forest skirt tipped
over her knee
wades through brambles
in seed-dusted air

Leaves on the hedges
tangled and dry
as insects' shed skin
brown as wind and sun
in the abandoned garden

How could she resist
the scent of the one
perfect dew-scented rose
red as spring as the tongue
touched to its petals

She pulls it free
because she will not
forgive it for being forbidden
nor is she shy to kiss the man
who challenges her there

And back in her family's
autumnal hall how could she
not think of the garden the rose
as a child begins to swell
the curve of her flesh

She knots her skirts again
returns through rain
that soaks the husks of summer
streaks of wet dust
in her damp hair

Where else another rose
to pull free
a man to taste danger with
a man she cannot have
unless she steals him

And so Janet at midnight
on All Hallows Eve calls the wind
to cover her passage
calls the oaks to hide her
the darkness to be her cloak

She waits at the crossroads
while the company passes
waits then pulls him free
holds him
though he changes in her arms

He twists like an adder fights
like a lion a bear still she holds
till he is just a man
and the falling sleet
curses them both in vain

Janet green and wild
her forest skirt
over her knee
wades through brambles
in the rain-dusted air

Leaves from the hedges rage
in the wind while she holds to the life
wrapped in her arms
in the man and the child
she holds close there

S TORY 4

so what if strangers
had the use of my
body—a simple
exchange, money paid
for a visit to

nothing of me, the
sea-stained shell that guards
me, within it I
slide free, glance out through
portholes with one-way

glass—they can't break through
no matter what they
touch, they can't reach through
to the part of me
where I laugh and live

Ravenous

how she leaves the house starving
for wind that thrusts the clouds
across lean sky   the grasses
that snarl around her
as she waits beneath leaves
and light the sun pours on her skin—

how she surges into
his red car   breath fervent
as ghosts caught by her thirst
at the drift of his hair in his eyes
the fever on her flesh
before he touches her—

how she yanks herself
into the self she makes
as she burns in her need to be fire
the passion to tear her throat
with her singing   to swallow
the world as it rings with glory—

how the pang in her belly twists
through her as his mouth leaves
her breasts   as he stretches above
her   wet with her his hands
plant at her sides in the sharp hollow moment
before he eases himself into her there—

how the great empty ache of her
watches alone in the park
as a boy learns to feed ducks
as a girl somersaults herself
down the rise   as a toddler learns
the ground beneath her feet—

how she watches the years behind her
trembling there as though
they could spill over her again
as if she could catch one and know
its flavour again through
simple singular desire—

how she still feels each
wrench in her gut
thundering for life   breath
how she could eat the world alive—
meaning how I could—
and how we would hunger still

RAIN IN THE FOREST

the leaves green light
   spills
      into the stream
with water thickened
   red by cedar
      it sings rain
over our hands
   disappears between
      the round stones below

I break a branch
   from the weedy maple
      to hold above you
the rain collects
   in large drops
      slow amplification
as the sun breaks
   through the fir
      and we're released

from a spell
   capering in puddles
      shaking our branch other branches
while the water collects
   on the soil too full
      to let it all go
it is this we remember
   this moment of surfeit
      while mist haloes your face

in a light sifted
   through alder and fir
      and more pure
for the journey
   green as the sword-fern
      as the damp air
rich as love
   and no way
      to leave you

SLEEPING WITH LAMBS

The woman is not mad
but she dreams about snow
piercing the windows of her house,
snow tunneling through the earth
to her cellar, moist flakes
already forming on the sheets
of her bed. Wind surrounds
the house like wolves,
sinewy as tree branches
etched into sleep. Not quite
the dream she expected: four
white heads tucked beside her
as she turns to see them there, neatly
beside her, the blankets folded just
under their chins, the air warm
with the wool of their breathing.

WOMAN IN BATH

Only in water is my skin
relieved; like Marat
water releases me. I can

remove the cloth that binds me
and breathe. Water
lines my skin like a

coffin's satin. Here I float
at ease, removed, a simple
leviathan in a pool, or

an embryo asleep in
a jar. Marat's bath empties
of blood and the oily

leakage from skin
and its putrefaction.
This is how water

eases the flesh,
how it holds all
our pain discards.

S TORY 5

All my life I fought
for breath, throat plugged with
my father's disdain,
clogged with my brother's
growing power. I

married to break the
clasp of mother's arms
and found myself her,
clutching my child in
a stifling house.

But now I watch my
husband: his gaunt chest
fights to pull in life
and air, grabbing for
sweet breath. Just like me.

Leaving Montana in August

Heat. Our last night
in this city. Sweat
and the sounds of the mill
and catfights from the window
above our bed. We've been
trading plans and memories
all night, the linen sheets
twisted between us.

We've said goodbye
to the Blackfoot River,
the Bitterroot Valley, the winter
wind from out the Hellgate,
dreaming of a green city, an ocean
a breeze that doesn't bring
stories and dust.

This place is too tangled
with the way we've built
our lives and failed,
always feeling as stifled
as in tonight's simmering heat.
But you can only blame a place
for not being home for so long
before you lose hold of
what home is. Summer
doesn't burn off as easily
as snow. Everything dies first.

But at six a.m. this is home
and beautiful. The sun rises
over Sentinel mountain, just as
distant thunder breaks from the sky.
First light pours onto our faces,
then rain scatters its blessing
on the sheets of our bed.
And we're ready, we're able
to start now again.

LUCIDITY

for Jan & Ray Brooks

Because there is nothing more sacred
    than the space between two words:
        translucent   leaves
    or the space between two visions:
        luminous leaves   leaden sky
they lie against each other. We fall between.
    Like the space we fall into
    between us.
It's early spring. We lie in our bed,
    you telling me the story you are. I hear
    your words stumble and flow
    like the rain trailing the glass—
    in the window above us the
        maple's new leaves   gray sky
    is enough to light them.
Because we are creating a new language
    words to bridge the distance between
        your back's curve   our vociferous sheets,
because the current, the spaces, the relation
    of the words are the gap between them.
Because we can talk all we want now
    our messages are opened
    by silence between.
Because the
        leaden sky, the
        leavened bread of our bed
    full of the dusk of us sleeping
    beside each other
        silent   speaking too much.
Because I woke before you,
    heard a word from your sleep, and I turned to you,
    your back, your shoulder blades
        translucent leaves
in the first early light of morning.
    We've fallen into a whole new world
    blessed by this
        green clarity   weighted sky.

V.   *Elemental: Water*

MAIRIE HAS DESSERT (AT 65)

Home all day now Jamie invades the
nervous house paces fills so much
space painting the air with sawdust
filing photographs in stacks maps
crawl across tables crackle under his
ink-stained finger pointing *there
let's go there* where the exotic can
become mundane Jamie has *time* to plan
hours to dedicate to sweet cedar to
organizing memories to seasoning our
lives with chatter about moving
somewhere anywhere to not be at home
but the power fails Jamie's eyes
flicker in candlelight we laugh &
carry votives upstairs the dog bounds
ahead of us we edge the cat to the
bed's foot & in our flannels we perch
pillows behind our backs prop books on
our bellies then lift chocolate to
our mouths giggling like children
reading aloud we own only ourselves &
no others ourselves & each other

MAIRIE IN THE EVENING (AT 75)

Upstairs hand in hand not frenzied as
at 20 or rushed as at 30 or warring
as at 40 or bored as at 50 or weary as
at 60 we leave on the light leave the
door open not whispered or silent I
don't flatten my belly nor does he we
can touch each other deliberately
from *there* to *there* to *there* always
familiar & new the cells that make
his body not the same my lips have
discovered before but the shape is
all remembered I would know him by
touch in the dark only his skin that
certain soap sweat dream masala only
his that thick fine mane wired with
grey only his spine curves that way
under my hand only his fingertips
know me so well it's as though they
designed me as I have made him we
move together so slowly in this
bright light we've all the time in
the world all the time in every world

PAPER ROCK SCISSORS STONE WATER AIR

Stone Water Air

I want to leave you but
you're sleeping so peacefully lashes
hit your cheek
just like the baby I imagine you were
skin luminous and
breaking with light
the fiery tone of muted
birth done in by
time
hour by hour grating
against your dreaming
that which is your self
pictured against flesh
you like this you're not
quite human yet
if that's why I'm going
with all this rawness
to burn me the reason and
route for leaving the
tale of us behind
if you turn it becomes
the tale of us together
for the first time and
I can't have that
I've gone to search the
world for bits of stone and the light
that's what I'll tell you

Paper Rock Scissors

wait the world holds water
they say it's water that will
save us the earth is
a perpetual motion machine
fueled by water and
where there is no water by
wind and what it makes of water's absence
sand I can almost feel the drop of
grit in my palm each tiny
grain against the fat
lush fall of rain it overwhelms
those desert seeds they swim
till I add more and they swallow
the water whole like some creature
starving for air they'll wonder
why I say this why I need
to trouble them with this story
why it's all just another
round of paper covers rock breaks
scissors cuts paper
sand wears the stone and
scissors down till they join
water dissolves the paper
while the rain is lost in dunes
dunes lost in sea and the
astonishment of the skin of my palm
open and waiting yes I can wait

DEATH IS AN AMPERSAND

> I think myself/death is an ampersand
> linking this word, that word/beyond the silence
> —Robin Skelton

Self-Portrait in Summer Rain   *As if a Body is What We Deserve*

my car winds like cable   that's how our spirit is born
around the lake and I am   locked and battened
looking for you   down in a ship's hold

rain dents   which is why we don't believe
the thin sheen of light on the road   in fairy tales
and I can't find you   the ship is launched and leaking

the lake is a void   in weathered water
to my right and I circle it   waves wash over the singular deck
like a plot I know I will enter   and spirit tries to break

once more around and   through for air
I stop the car but   while the heart sings
with no sign of you   a shanty about work and continuance

I fold my jacket   and the wind tears at the sails
on the car seat   it's a rough sea for spirit
slip the keys into my pocket   lying heavy on the hull

rain pebbles the lake   its weight is ballast
and I step into it   trying trying to make the ship rise
solid as night itself   above the water line

small waves tug my clothes   but we can't believe in magic
like your hands   because there is no way out
and I swim out   of the witch's oven

I can hear   because the apple is so poisonous
nothing but dark water   it burns our mouths away
the token drift of your voice because there is no noble prince

in my head   hacking a way through the thorns
I can feel myself   because we're still in the dark woods
thinning out in the cloud   and can't see out

of black rain   into happily ever after
meeting the water   happily ever after
and you in the night   happily ever after

TUPPENCE IN POCKET

When I touch the coin you gave me you're there, tossing sticks
for bats to swoop at, high into the thick humid air
as we walk along the river path near the iron bridge
in the late summer night. What you tell me is true:
the bats fly at them, deceived. They think they're alive,
dance all directions, chasing nothing in the dark.

I remember another time, even longer ago, dark
summer-night again, your father screaming words like sticks
he would use to beat you. His anger something alive.
I was waiting for you at the door—the dense air
thick with lies—I saw then what was between you, the true
hatred between you, was the only bridge.

I wasn't used to that. I thought family love was a bridge
that would carry me over the bad world, over every dark
place in my life and I suppose that for me it was true.
But you had a family where love was harm, home only sticks,
so you got away, where you could breathe the air
freely without them, where you could study a way to live.

Before you fled the coast where I still live
we left magic in the silent woods there, coins to bridge
time—the silly statues you'd made at camp—we left them to air
in the forest rains at a cedar's base, buried their feet dark
in the loam. Strange things to set among the sticks
and leaves, but they were a way to make your leaving true.

The stories of our adventures are wild but true
even if new friends can't believe the tales. We live
different lives, but something between us sticks
no matter how long we're apart, we're able to bridge
the time like nothing. We know the secrets, know the dark
parts of each other's lives, know how to make them disappear like air.

100

One night in a church courtyard, you sang me an English air
about a woman promised to a boy, how their marriage became true,
but of course he died. I know it's a tale that's dark
but beautiful too and it helps me to make sense of how we live.
That song, the statues, small things that are gifts to bridge
all the changes, the years, the hates and loves—they're what sticks.

They're stubborn as we are, and as true. They're the gathered sticks
we throw into the deceptive air, the coin you gave me on the bridge
fingered rich with memory, dark with age, that we spend to live.

FIVE. *Where She Ends*

REMNANTS 6

M. June Fisher
1900?-1981

items in my home

junior gymnastics trophy dated 1913
photograph of her dancing dated 1919
white gold wedding ring dated 1921
oriental rug
crystal brandy snifters
a sable tail
small compact w/ Parrish "Contentment"
silver candlesticks
green silk slip
creme-coloured teddy
pearls (faux)
letters
small square saucepan

small heavy nugget of dental gold

BENEATH THE SIGN MARKED *MAIDENS 9 >*

my mother and I stubbornly face
north the sign points south we pose
and grin Dad doesn't get it then
snaps us frozen into time there
maiden   wife   crone
I am Janus facing the future
constructing myself while I still
suffer the girl I was the maiden the
young woman writing my life from the
middle here I remember the *truth* of
days past walking the beach with my
father with my friends with my
husband picking up shells for their
stinking weight their wicked beauty
so flawless they must be *made* so
perfect no one could devise such a
treasure unearthed with my sharp
eyes with my nimble hands with my
hazed eyes with my twigged hands
she dares to step into the tide to delve
for them deeper, I dare to step into
the tide old woman you dare to step
into the tide you let me create you

WOMAN AT THE EDGE OF THE WORLD

Sometimes I'm there on the Victory Stage
dancing with my young arms open. Sometimes
I watch my daughters' father die
as though he were turning from me.

I will say what I want to.
Anger bites out from me like an animal
guarding her young. But my young aren't young
and have children. My daughters have daughters

and so they go on leaving me here.
It is myself I guard.
My body has been crumbling for years and the pain
eats me inside out. I bear it.

Sometimes I wake naked in the hallway.
Sometimes bruised or burned
and they want to take me from these rooms
with their wood and comfort.

My mother's furniture here. The thick bright
familiar rugs, things my daughters want.
There is nothing here I leave them, not my rooms,
my rings, the names I chose for them, not the things

I bought to be theirs. All I leave them
is these old bones. And not my vixen's love.
That I keep for my own.

STORYTELLER TALKING AT THE END OF HER DAYS

So what is paradise, since we yearn
for it so unevenly and think we touch
it but so fleetingly it is brief as the touch
of the dream's finger to our lips as we sleep
When you read my words to me they escape me.

Paradise seems like hell to me, all that lying
in the sun and sweating lazy sex.
I like mine in a colder climate where
the only warmth is what we ourselves
can generate between us and call passion: the heat
of our bodies coming alive between us.
I know I wander somewhat when I speak; it's because
my mind entertains so many guests—each thought
reminds me of another and they all crowd
in at once too quickly to separate so I embrace
them all. Sure I've travelled had lovers
married had a child and dreams
wrote some of them down. Sometimes I got lost
in the tangle, locked to a place a time
and wrote it down, broke away to follow
another thread. A myriad of voices
woven with my own, singing a madrigal
of light, each note a point in the woven sky.
My favourite memories are the most simple—
sitting at night on the chesterfield, the rest
of the house asleep, the cat beside me. I
touched her face as though it were mine.
There isn't much I would do again
if I could. I haven't yet let go
of it all in my mind. I can unlock it at will
but it all floods in, more than I can control.
I always used to like the feeling of having
more in my hands than I could control.
I used to like dangerous men but the ordinary
was the best, when the spark of feeling
between us wasn't just pride,
and we weren't afraid to let
ourselves be taken... enough of the flesh
for now it holds me.

I feel I haven't lived enough have lived
too much have lived on fire trying to dance
so fast the flames would not burn. And now
I'm lying in a snow field flush with the
earth; it's cold but I can see the tangle
of stars in the sky and a few are falling.
Yes it's true, each one is a small ball
of fire like the sun but a few are falling.

WHAT COMES OF WINTER

Harvest is past: the feasts and long
preparations for winter

over. Herbs hang in the rafters;
apples slowly wrinkle in straw.

The frosted stones along the roadways
burn chill into the traveller's bones.

Dark sends us closer to home.
Even the cat, the wanderer

warrior queen, curls by the fire
her back to the changing wind.

Sleep pulls her into
the hollow of November.

Days seem ordered
as stars.

Our calm shadows in the dim light,
drifting through

the washing of sheets, the making
of beds. Stew bubbles

in the pot. Its welcome scent
bumps against the walls,

its sullen music
a charm against the wind's

angry song. I had forgotten
this stillness tumbling us

into dreams more real
than the method of our days,

the chaos of sleep
raw and desperate as though

this is the way the world has
to grab hold in us and live.

KILMARNOCK JEANNIE

She owned rain that poured from
   the bowl of her hands,
sparked like mica
   in the flight of her greyed hair,
caught light and held it
   while she herself
was long hidden back
   in the mess of leaves.

She owned a house built of nests
   and twigs stolen
from thickets, boards
   from the building lot,
the barest shield against the eyes
   that caught
her firelight, that crooned to her
   from the trees.

She owned scars dark with dirt
   and distance,
the stories they told
   that she would not.
She told only fortunes, dreams
   that muttered her,
lines sketching her eyes that sang of
   each mile a day holds.

She owned dust that covered
   the rags of her shoes
her feet hardened with travel
   the gnarled gap
of leather and skin, but above that
   the arc of her ankles
like wings, Mercury, a message
   of grace, of travel, of ruin.

STORY 6

For Liliane & Cyril Welch

What we do is climb,
love, rise above the
jumble of binding
towns and roads, to the
places where trust is

all, a bond so twined
between us it's more
taut than rope or our
muscles as we still
move upwards learning

once again how to
trust our forged bodies
against the shape of
all the slopes we've climbed.
The journey is all.

Meditation at La Push

Sky swells over land
cloud curdles above wide, wide sea
goes on forever, almost   here
                                                   in the foreground a man walks by
                                                   and I wonder what it's like
                                                   to inhabit that face, those clothes.
                                                   I can feel his stiff jeans creasing
                                                   open, folding against my skin
                                                   as he paces away. Ocean out into
nothing   everything   no difference.
The wide wider widest expanse bracketed
by rock by tide. I want to mark that ocean.
To place its mark on me. I want
to be someone everyone no one
swallowed by sky. Beach trail. Gulls.
Broken, silvery logs. Scrub on the foreshore,
rank with summer. The white agitation
of waves broken by rock and the line
that wavers between sea sky sea.
The rock I chose all green
and the barnacle like Mount Rainier.   We are out of time.
                                        Waves crash steadier than
                                        traffic on the interstate,
                                        merely noise. I worry
                                        that I would not recognize wonder
                                        if I stumbled on it—or awe,
                                        raw   open   gathering
                                        Sea roars against the still line
                                        of horizon and if I walked out
                                        toward it—if I stumbled
                                        over the bumpy furrows—that line
                                        would recede before me.
                      And is it wonder
or calculation as my mind
turns over like an engine
starting to devour the world of its making:
despair is such an easy belief, but
light striking through the sea spray
near my face still strikes me
dumb. And it isn't hopeless to think

of my name written in the sand
above the tide where someone
pronounces it wrong, but still I stir,
dreaming recognizing my name as mine.
That is wonder.   So many stones I see on the beach
                                   and I can't stop thinking of each
                                   one: this stone is a world. Continents
                                   and ocean. A million
                                   other worlds, and the sand of destroyed
                                   worlds between them
                                   like dust between stars. Our history is
                                   just one of those sand grains, not even
                                   a world and yet
                                   I can hear us teeming all over the
                                   planet, standing on beaches,
                                   piling up stones.
How this stone would slide past my lips: sun warmed,
a few grains of sand falling, the salt,
its wave-smoothed presence heavy on my tongue,
how it would clink against my teeth,
shuddering my jaw. And then
how I would swallow it.
warm round weight stretching down my throat—
each inch aware
as it sinks into my belly. A stone there.
                                   The line of surf breaking into foam. The
                                   single tree, water washes 'round
                                   its smoothed trunk and roots. Waves rocking
                                   the huge stumps.
                                   I am tired of caution.
                                   I walk right into the sea.

You designed the map
This is not a test

beyond *happily*
ever after   you're
forest-deep in the
thick of real life   not
the dreaming child now

who ached for her life
to just *start*   this is
the promised land where
you know the worn trail's
every bend   to

duck branches   clamber
across deadfalls   edge
around arabesques
of roots   navigate
the undergrowth's green

archipelagos
the familiar
sodden lurch through the
creek and the climb to
the view that spans to

low hills and the strait
and the white snow caps
beyond   this place that
you thought was no where
is now here   now *here*

VI.   *Elemental: An Epilogue*

SHEELA-NA-GIG

Her round bald pate, encircled
eyes, nose triangular,
her mouth a small vee

of hinted smile—
she's laughing, deadly earnest,
from the eaves

of Kilpeck's saintly church.
Amongst the corbels'
beasts and hunting dogs,

predator or prey
she's part of that hunt,

so defiantly female
centuries of vicars
left her untouched.

Her mockery,
serious as breath,
answers the question

where are we going:
where we come from.

Spindle legs bent,
arms curled under,

fingers bent and opening
the mouth of that cave,

holding its secrets
open to the world,
no less mysterious

for all of its blatancy,
those fingers almost daring us
to go inside, go inside

where everything revealed
is also swallowed,

where the opening
is also a labyrinth.

This figure has the comic
forbiddenness of the word:
cunt. The hard-edged

beginning and end
with the interior
to get lost in.

The giving of power
adds to this power.
All the insult and all of the envy.

The welcoming toothless *teeth*
of such passive victory,

the open beckoning mouth of fate
swallowing us whole
innocent of motive, weaponless,

faithless, her laughter
owning us all.

A COURSE IN SADNESS

or: *henry's landscape*

what is closest passes most quickly
what is farther is slow and lasts

while the train rides the ridgeline
the land travels beyond us, blurred
behind the details of my hand etched
against the glass: the song's flow
behind my words, behind the windows we look beyond—

a rise we inhabit, as clumps of spring grasses
knot against the side of the track
a noisy punctuation, the shuffle-bang wheels,
while the line of the hill dips,
the distance bending long slow notes—

a clutch of trees in green rain
the spark of sun in the marrow that fires
before it melds into the undergrowth,
a hollow sound, sad but clear—

and the horizon's rise and fall
draws the story to your fingers
smoothing then waking
the strings of your guitar
into what is more than grief: not anger but passion—

it doesn't make it happy
but it finds its voice and sings, henry, sings

MAIRIE AT NIGHT (AT 85)

I lie in my narrow bed alone like a
child can't sleep though my eyes burn
with it a clock ticks mechanic and
loud binding me to each second I
breathe in the space between I
breathe as though it's my job it's
what I was born to do the sheets are
scented with sun just like when my
mother hung them on the line to dry I
did that too in Jamie's bed who has
done this for me I can't remember
Ellen or Ben or someone else the
blankets are heavy it feels like work
to hold them up to be a presence here
to stop the clock ticking through
emptiness to notice its sound the
sheet's freshness the blankets'
weighted existence the room needs
someone to see pictures in the dark I
cannot see something bright now moves
in the darkness *there* Jamie's gone
ahead & I'm ready to catch him up now

M AIRIE AT MIDNIGHT

the smells of breakfast of Bessie of
the sun on the fields the fire in the
hearth a reek from the stalls knifes
in my nose I hate morning & the scent
of exhaust & bitter coffee I tear
garden basil to wake it & its scent
prickles me aware here's Jamie Ellen
Ben for this moment here & bright all
circled smiling in the window's lemon
light Ellen's perfume Ben's socks
mint tea & an ink-dusty book
woodsmoke & incense crackers & wine
sawdust sweet cedar seasoning our
lives only Jamie's skin has that
certain soap sweat dream masala the
sheets scented with sun & the clock
ticking ticking ticking the scent of
oatmeal warms the room Jamie Ellen
Ben Jamie Ellen Ben Jamie Ellen Ben
Mairie Mairie Mairie *there* goodnight

A CKNOWLEDGMENTS

I would like to thank the editors of the following magazines where these poems first appeared, sometimes in earlier versions.

THE ALSOP REVIEW (www.alsopreview.com): "Anything You Say," "The Basement Exit," "A Course in Sadness," "Furious," "The Game of Cards," "Gravestones At Elgin Cathedral," "Paper Rock Scissors Stone Water Air," "Ravenous," "Sleeping With Lambs," "Story 1," "Storyteller Talking At The End Of Her Days," "Tuppence in Pocket," "You Designed the Map"
THE ANTIGONISH REVIEW: "The Lovers in Grey"
ARC, "Beneath The Sign Marked *Maidens > 9*," "Lucidity," "Meditation At La Push," "Ravenous," "The Tree in The World," *"Winter or Goodbye"* (part iv of "The Lovers in Grey")
ARIEL: "The Name Of The Hunt"
CANADIAN LITERATURE: "Anything You Say," "Delicate As The Shapes of Spirits," "The Prophet as Traveller"
CONTEMPORARY VERSE 2: "Alchemical Daughter"
DANDELION: "The Man's Dark Voice"
DESCANT: "Sleeping With Lambs"
EARTH'S DAUGHTERS (U.S.A.): *"I Was a Pagan Baby"* (part ii of "The World Of The Dead"
GRAIN: "Tuppence in Pocket"
LITRAG (U.S.A.): "Consider Teiresias"
LYNX (www.bath.ac.uk/~exxdgdc/lynx.html): "Ways To Transcend The Spiritual"
MISSISSIPPI MUD (U.S.A.): "Parable of the Headwaters"
NeWEST: "Sooke River Story"
THE NEW QUARTERLY: "Leaving Montana in August" (as "Heat & the City"), "Woman In Bath"
ODYSSEY (England): "Furious"
POET LORE (U.S.A.): "The Game of Cards," "Loving The Green Man"
POETRY NEWSLETTER: "Ways To Transcend The Spiritual"
QUARRY: "Tam Lin"
STAR*LINE (U.S.A.): "Map Of The Ancient World," "My Love Out Riding"
TICKLE ACE: "What Comes Of Winter"
THE WINDSOR REVIEW: "Story 3" (as "Story 1"), "Woman At The Edge Of The World"

Three of these poems have been finalists in ARC's Poem of the Year contests and each was published as an Editor's Choice: "Lucidity" in 1997, "Ravenous" in 1998, and "Beneath The Sign Marked *Maidens > 9*" in 1999. "Storyteller

Talking At The End Of Her Days" was a finalist in the 1990 National Poetry Contest and appeared in *More Garden Varieties II*. "Gravestones At Elgin Cathedral" was a finalist in the 1992 contest and appeared in *Vintage 92*.

"There As Here There Are No Doors" appeared in *A Discord of Flags: Canadian Poets Write About the Gulf War*. "*Alban Eilir*: A Calling-On Song" appeared in *Something More Than Words* an anthology in honour of Robin Skelton. "The Tree In The World" also appeared in *We All Begin in a Little Magazine: Arc and the Promise of Canada's Poets, 1978 to 1998*. "Reconstructing A Life" appeared as part of the essay "Poetry as DNA" in *Reinventing Memory*, and was reprinted in *Imprints and Casualties: Selected Readings from the Living Archives of the Feminist Caucus of the League of Canadian Poets*, both edited by Anne Burke. Poems from this collection were also published in the limited-edition chapbook, *Sheela-na-Gig*.

I would like to thank my family and friends for their stories, inspiration, and encouragement, especially Christina & Matt DeCoursey and Shelagh & John Graham. John Barton, Marilyn Bowering, Jan Brooks, Rita Donovan. Gail Dubrow, Ruth Brinton, Vicki Ford, and James Gurley gave me invaluable editorial advice. Thanks to Susan Ehrens, author of *A Poetic Vision: The Photographs of Anne Brigman* for her help in obtaining permission for and access to "The Storm Tree." My gratitude and thanks to John Buschek of BuschekBooks for his enthusiasm, commitment, and editorial vision.

I am grateful to Artists Trust of Washington, the King County Arts Commission, and the Seattle Arts Commission for support during the writing of these poems.

IM: Sylvia Skelton, Robin Skelton, Charles Lillard.

ABOUT THE AUTHOR

Neile Graham grew up in Victoria, British Columbia. She currently lives in Seattle and works at the University of Washington. Her poetry, short fiction, reviews, and articles have been published in American, British, and Canadian literary journals and anthologies. Her first collection of poetry, *Seven Robins* (Penumbra Press) appeared in 1983. Her second, *Spells for Clear Vision* (Brick Books), was shortlisted for the 1994 Pat Lowther Award for the best book of poems by a Canadian woman. She has received grants from the Canada Council, Artists Trust, and the Seattle, King County, and Washington State arts commissions. She is hard at work on a novel based on the "Gypsy Davey" ballad, and a new collection of poems about her travels in Scotland. The Bumbershoot Arts Festival schedule describes her work as: "breathtaking and stern, abducting her audience into a realm of disturbing yet beautiful detail and experience."